Treating Wastewater

Flush!

Treating Wastewater

by Karen Mueller Coombs
photographs by Jerry Boucher

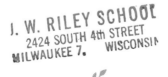
Carolrhoda Books, Inc./Minneapolis

For Dad and Viva, with love...

The publisher would like to thank Dennis Lindeke and Patricia Oates, Metropolitan Council Wastewater Services (Minnesota).

Carolrhoda Books, Inc. c/o The Lerner Group
241 First Avenue North, Minneapolis, Minnesota 55401

LIBRARY OF CONGRESS CATALOGING-IN-PUBLICATION INFORMATION

Coombs, Karen Mueller.

Flush! : treating wastewater / by Karen Mueller Coombs ; photographs by Jerry Boucher.
p. cm.
Includes index.
ISBN 0-87614-879-8
1. Sewage disposal—Juvenile literature. 2. Sewage disposal plants—Juvenile literature. [1. Sewage disposal.] I. Boucher, Jerry, ill. II. Title.
TD646.C69 1995
628.3—dc20
94-37676
CIP
AC

Manufactured in the United States of America

1 2 3 4 5 6 – JR – 00 99 98 97 96 95

Special thanks to Lee Cory, Operations Manager of the Encina Water Pollution Control Facility at Carlsbad, California, for allowing me to tour the plant while it was under construction; to Mike Hogan, Operations Superintendent of the Encina Plant, for the time he took in showing me the plant and explaining its operation; to Steve Bagwell, Legislative Manager of the Water Environment Federation, for answering my numerous questions; to the members of my writing group, Kathleen Chambers, Nancy Elliott, Edith Fine, Judith Josephson, Stephanie McPherson, and Marie Shephard, for their willingness to hear more about wastewater treatment processes than they probably cared to; and most of all, to my husband, Jon, for explaining the processes to me, and for his patient readings of the work-in-progress.

—K. M. C.

Thanks to Linda Henning, Pauline Langsdorf, Dennis Lindeke, Patricia Oates, Steve Wareham, Steven Stark, William Moeler, Rick Thompson, Leo Hermes, Richard Kraft, and Mark Pavlick of Metropolitan Council Wastewater Services; Bruce Henning, Lemna Corporation; Rod Perteron and Bruce Degerman of Barron, Wisconsin, Wastewater Treatment; and Ken Belargion of Amery, Wisconsin, Wastewater Treatment.

—J. B.

Metric Conversion Chart		
When You Know:	*Multiply by:*	*To Find:*
feet	0.3	meters
miles	1.61	kilometers
square miles	2.59	square kilometers
pounds	0.45	kilograms
gallons	3.79	liters

Contents

Introduction

Water, More Precious than Gold

We can live for weeks without food, but for only a few days without water. Water is our most valuable natural resource. But less than one percent of the earth's water is usable. That's because most water—ninety-seven percent—is ocean water. It is too salty for drinking, growing food, or use in industry. The rest of the earth's water, about three percent, is freshwater. More than two-thirds of that is frozen in icecaps, icebergs, or glaciers. That leaves less than one percent for us to use, most of it under the ground or in rivers and lakes. And that one percent has to be used again and again. It is important to use this water wisely, and when it's dirty, to clean it well.

This wastewater treatment plant returns water to a nearby river.

Water dirtied from household and industry use is called sewage or **wastewater.** Wastewater is full of things that go down a drain, things like human waste, chemicals from household cleaners and pesticides, pieces of paper and plastic, bits of food, and left-over drinks. Wastewater is cleaned at a wastewater treatment plant. These plants are usually built near **waterways** (oceans, rivers, lakes, or streams) so there is some place to put the water when it is returned to the environment.

Polluted water can make life difficult for people who make a living on the water.

Untreated wastewater pollutes the waterways. Polluted water kills fish, wildlife, and plants. It destroys swimming, boating, and fishing areas, and spreads disease to people who drink the water. Treating wastewater before it goes into the waterways helps protect people and the environment. Wastewater treatment is a very important job.

Out the Window

A History of Wastewater Treatment

The early method of getting rid of wastewater—dumping it out the window—was not pleasant for the people down below.

Wastewater treatment plants have been around only since the late 1800s. Before then, each civilization handled sewage in its own way. Four thousand years ago, some ancient civilizations had simple toilets and drainage systems. Around A.D. 100, the Romans even had faucets, as well as pipes to carry wastes away. When Rome lost its power, plumbing got worse. People everywhere began dumping their wastewater and garbage into the gutters and ditches, or sometimes out an open window. The wastes then flowed into the nearest ocean, river, lake, stream, or pond.

There were fewer people then, so in time, nature itself could clean the wastewater. Once in the waterway, the wastes became diluted, or watered down, and after a while, settled to the bottom. Today, however, with many more people, nature alone can't handle all of the wastewater.

Holes in the Ground

During the 1800s, most people had backyard outhouses. Unlike modern toilets, an outhouse used no water—this small, wooden building sat above a deep hole in the ground.

Some outhouses had a metal pail under the wooden bench seat to catch the wastes. The pails were then emptied into a large container in the ground called a cesspit. From the cesspit, the waste was spread on soil as fertilizer. Although this worked well to help crops grow, people didn't know that the waste was full of **microorganisms,** tiny life-forms that we can't even see. Some of the microorganisms are harmful germs that often cause diseases.

An outhouse usually had a wooden bench seat inside with a round opening cut in it.

You may be familiar with this modern form of the outhouse.

Improvement Begins

Outhouses are still used in many parts of the world, including some rural areas of North America. They were common here even after an early type of toilet called the water closet came into use. Invented in England in the late 1700s, the water closet had a tank high above it that flushed water down into the toilet, washing wastes through a pipe to a cesspit. Unfortunately, these early toilets did not work very well.

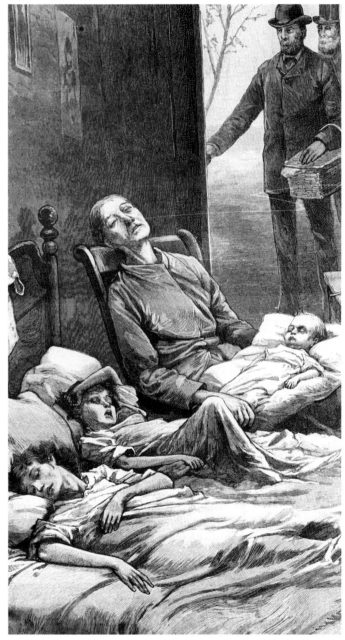

Typhoid fever often struck an entire family.

Cities grew. More people flushed more wastewater into cesspits. The cesspits began to overflow, sometimes seeping into wells used for drinking water. Thousands of people died from typhoid fever and cholera. Nobody knew that polluted water caused these diseases.

Then in the mid-1800s, a French chemist, Louis Pasteur, discovered that certain microorganisms can make people ill. Finally scientists realized that raw sewage was dangerous. So instead of sending waste to the cesspits, people began connecting water closet pipes to the underground pipes that had been set up to carry rainwater. This kept the wastewater out of people's wells, but now all of this sewage began flowing into lakes, ponds, rivers, and oceans.

Louis Pasteur's scientific discoveries have helped save thousands of lives.

Headway and Horrors

As inventors improved on the water closet in the late 1800s and more people had running water, water closets became more practical and less expensive. Flush toilets were no longer just for rich people, and they became more and more common in England and the United States. But raw sewage was still pouring into the waterways. Finally in 1886, New York City built the first wastewater treatment plant to keep the sewage from ruining the beaches of Coney Island.

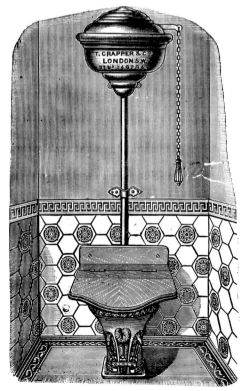

CRAPPER'S

Improved

Registered Ornamental

Flush-down W.C.

With New Design Cast-iron Syphon Water Waste Preventer.

No 518.

Improved Ornamental Flush-down W.C. Basin (Registered No. 145,823), Polished Mahogany Seat with flap, New Pattern 3-gallon Cast-iron Syphon Cistern (Rd. No. 149,284), Brass Flushing Pipe and Clips, and Pendant Pull, complete as shown £6 15 0

The polluted New York Harbor in 1883 (above)

Englishman Thomas Crapper is credited with improving the water closet (or w.c.). This advertisement (left) shows one of his toilets.

In the decades following, thousands of plants were built, but they weren't able to keep up with all the wastewater. By the 1960s, millions of gallons of raw sewage, along with poisonous metals and chemicals from factories, were flowing into the waterways. Between 1952 and 1969, the Cuyahoga (ky-uh-HO-guh) River in Cleveland, Ohio, became so filthy that it often caught on fire. Once it burned for eight days. People living near the river marched in the streets and wrote angry letters demanding that the river be cleaned up.

The polluted Cuyahoga River on fire in 1952

Enough Is Enough

The burning river and the angry people forced the United States government into action, and in 1977 it added the Clean Water Act to the law. This act says the country has to clean its wastewater before returning it to the environment. The government set aside billions of dollars to help cities build new plants and to improve old ones.

A wastewater treatment plant under construction in Boston, Massachusetts

15

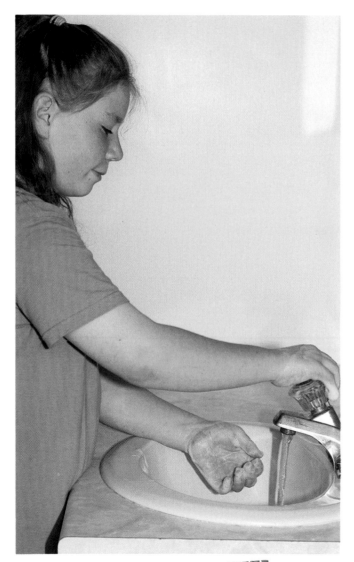

2

Down the Drain

Preliminary Treatment

Clean water that flows from a tap or into a toilet comes from a water treatment plant, where it has been purified for drinking and household use. Then after it is used, it goes down a drain. With all the flushing, drinking, washing, bathing, cooking, and cleaning we do, each person in the United States sends between 50 and 100 gallons of wastewater down the drain every day. Thirty-three percent of that comes from flushing toilets. In most cities and towns, this used household water ends up at the local wastewater treatment plant. How does it get there?

When you flush a toilet, the water drains into a sewer pipe under the building. The pipe is called a service line. In homes, water from the sinks, washing machine, dishwasher, and other drains in the house flows into the service line, too.

Pictured above is a **septic system** under construction. When a house has a septic system, the water goes only a little farther than the service line, which leads to a septic tank buried in the yard. The tank is connected to pipes filled with holes, and waste is filtered out as the water dribbles through crushed rock or gravel and into the ground.

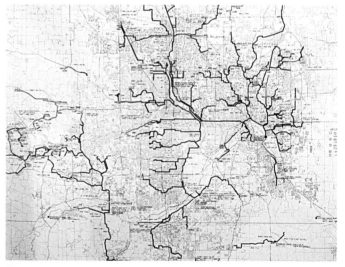

Wastewater often travels through miles of underground sewer pipes before it reaches the treatment plant.

The service line leads to a larger pipe, called a main line, under the street nearby. Pipes from all the homes on the street join the main line. Only wastewater from homes and businesses runs through this line, so it's called a sanitary or separate sewer.

Five hundred miles of pipes serve the Minneapolis and St. Paul area in Minnesota.

In some cities, rainwater, melted snow, sprinkler and irrigation water, even water from people washing their cars runs into the main line. Then it's called a combined sewer.

It's often a long way to the plant, so other main sewer lines may join into an even bigger line. Sometimes this line is as big as eight or ten feet across. Finally, the water arrives at the wastewater treatment plant.

Grease from household kitchens forms balls in the sewer pipes.

Different Treatment Plants, Same Smell

Each wastewater treatment plant is different in size, in equipment, and even in the types of treatments it uses. The more people and businesses there are in an area, the bigger and more complicated the plant must be. In large plants, workers each have different jobs. The plant manager is in charge, operators run the plant's equipment, maintenance workers keep the equipment running properly, and laboratory technicians test the water to make sure it's getting clean. In a small plant, the same person might do all of these jobs.

Mark, a lab technician at a large treatment plant, checks the amount of solid material in wastewater.

These carbon filters clean the air at this treatment plant.

At different stages of treatment, wastewater can smell like fish or skunk, or like rotten cabbage, meat, or eggs. Sometimes special equipment can actually take the bad smell out of the air. At some plants, a huge cover over the equipment keeps the smell inside. At other plants, you'll probably want to hold your nose.

21

The bar screen acts like a strainer, stopping anything too large to flow past it.

Caught on the Bars

The odor in the bar screen room, the first treatment step in most plants, is the same as in a bathroom when the toilet is plugged. But it's one of the most interesting places in the treatment plant. Here, objects flushed into the sewer by accident or on purpose are removed from the water.

The untreated water, called **influent,** flows into a large concrete channel. The bar screen stands in the middle of this channel. As the brownish green wastewater passes through, the screen catches any large solid objects floating in the sewage. This includes human waste, wads of toilet paper, disposable diapers, plastics, rags, small toys, false teeth, jewelry, sometimes even paper money.

If the water comes from a combined sewer, the screen also catches sticks or rubber balls that have fallen down the sewer. Some bar screens have caught dead—and sometimes live—turtles, eels, and snakes.

Periodically, a large rake is lowered to the bottom of the screen and scrapes all the trapped material upward and off the bars. This material is then hauled to a landfill and buried.

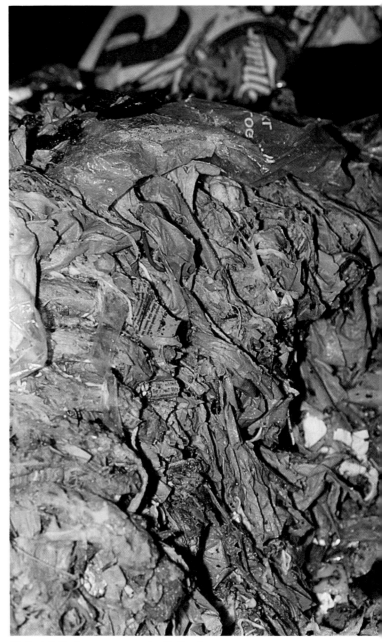

Material that was scraped off the bar screen

The bar screen catches some interesting objects.

OD[ ]OUS AIR

Out with the Nitty Gritty

Everything that slips past the screen flows into a deep concrete tank about the size of a small room. The tank is called a grit chamber—here, grit is removed from the water. Some grit is material like sand, material that was never alive. This is **inorganic matter.** Grit that comes from once-living plants and animals, like seeds and coffee grounds, is **organic matter.**

This machine (opposite page) carries grit from the grit chamber to the red bin below it (right). The blue pipe above the bin sucks out "odorous air" (smelly air) and sends it to the carbon filters shown on page 21.

If you've ever filled a bucket with dirty water and left it standing, you've made a grit chamber. Because grit is heavier than the other materials in the water, it sinks. When the grit hits the bottom of the grit chamber, it's pumped out, washed, and taken to a landfill, along with solids from the bar screen.

The water leaving the grit chamber doesn't look much different than when it went in. It's still a murky, muddy green, because only the large, solid materials have been removed. The water is still full of harmful microorganisms, and part of a wastewater treatment plant's job is to remove as many of these as possible.

Scum and Sludge

Primary Treatment

The water gets its first real cleaning during the next treatment step, **primary treatment.** When wastewater leaves the grit chamber, it still has a lot of small, solid matter floating in it. Most of it is very light organic matter—human waste.

To remove as much of this solid matter as possible, the wastewater flows into a primary clarifier (KLAR-uh-fy-er), sometimes called a sedimentation (seh-duh-men-TAY-shun) tank.

The water sits quietly for about two hours in this deep tank. As it sits, the heaviest material settles to the bottom, much as it did in the grit chamber. Most of the human waste settles, but some lightweight matter—grease, foam, oil, hair, and light pieces of rubber and plastic—floats on top.

This floating material has its own name: scum. Blades skim the scum from the surface of the water in the primary clarifier. These blades, which look like gigantic windshield wipers, push the scum out of the tank. Then the scum is pumped out and hauled to a landfill.

The matter that settles to the bottom of the clarifier is called **sludge.** Giant blades under the water also scrape sludge off the bottom of the tank. The sludge will be treated separately from the water, which now looks less brown, but not nearly as clean as swimming pool water.

Primary treatment removes about 40 to 50 percent of the solids from the wastewater. This water is not yet safe enough to use. The Clean Water Act requires **secondary treatment,** a level of treatment after the primary stage. Nevertheless, 15 percent of all plants return the water to the waterway after primary treatment.

More treatment means more equipment, which costs a lot of money. Some cities cannot afford the costs of improving their treatment plants. Sometimes the federal government takes a city to court to force it to add secondary treatment.

Some treatment plants recycle the oil they clean from the wastewater in the primary clarifier.

An aeration basin

Bubble, Bubble, Munch, Munch

Secondary Treatment

In 85 percent of plants, the water now begins its secondary treatment. The water flows into another huge concrete tank, called an aeration (air-AY-shun) basin. Aeration means adding air to something, similar to blowing bubbles through a straw into a glass of milk.

On the bottom of the basin are dozens of little nozzles that squirt tiny air bubbles into the water.

This boy is aerating his milk.

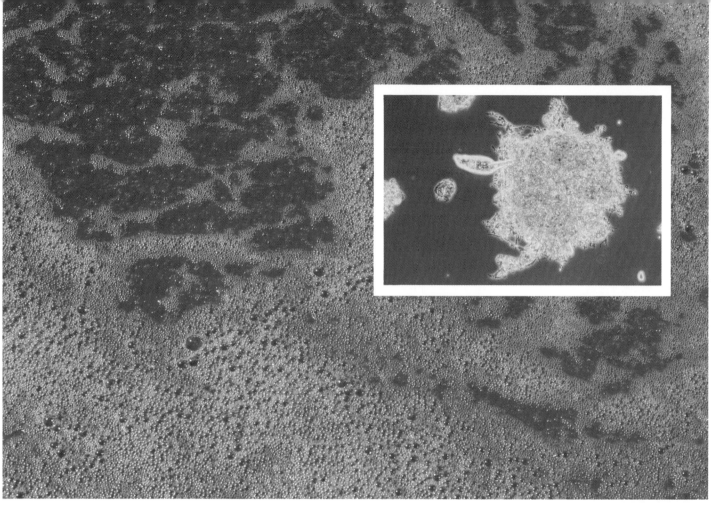

Bubbles in the aeration basin (above). *A close-up view of helpful aerobic bacteria* (inset), *as seen through a microscope*

The air bubbles in the aeration basin add oxygen to the water, which helps the millions of useful microorganisms that are naturally present in the wastewater. Not all microorganisms are harmful—some actually help in treating the water. They are **bacteria,** the wriggly creatures you see when you look at a drop of pond water under a microscope. They're called **aerobic** (uh-RO-bik) **bacteria** because, like people, they need oxygen. The oxygen gets them moving so they can help clean up the organic matter still in the water.

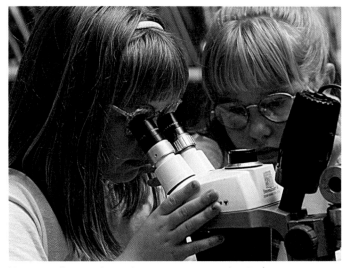
You usually need a microscope to see bacteria.

We can see bacteria from the aeration basin without a microscope.

In a treatment plant, bacteria are nature's vacuum cleaners. The aerobic bacteria in the aeration basin surround dissolved organic matter (mostly from human waste) and absorb it—they suck it into their bodies. As the bacteria eat, they change the waste into carbon dioxide (a harmless, odorless gas) and water. Then they multiply by splitting into more pieces. Soon there are billions of them. The bacteria will keep eating and splitting as long as there is organic matter and oxygen in the water.

As they eat, the bacteria get fatter and keep multiplying. If you held a jar of wastewater up to the light, you could see them without a microscope. They look like clumps of lumpy oatmeal hanging in the water.

Sinking Bacteria

After three to six hours, the aerobic bacteria finish feasting on all the waste in the aeration basin. Then the wastewater, full of fat bacteria, flows into the next tank, where it will stay for four to seven hours. This large concrete tank is called the secondary clarifier or sedimentation tank.

The fat bacteria are very heavy. They sink lower and lower in the tank, and finally settle on the bottom. They've become sludge.

The fat bacteria sink to the bottom of the secondary clarifier.

Brown, bacteria-filled water enters the secondary clarifier from the center of the tank (below) and begins to settle to the bottom (right). By the time the water reaches the outside edge of the tank (below right), it is much cleaner than when it went in.

With no more food to eat, the bacteria get hungry. Some of the sludge gets pumped back into the aeration basin, so the bacteria can start eating, multiplying, and growing again. The rest of the sludge then moves on to another piece of equipment.

What Happens to All That Sludge?

Almost half of the money spent in a plant goes toward treating and getting rid of sludge, also called biosolids. First, water is removed from the sludge. This can be done by letting the smelly sludge settle like grit, by forcing it to float like scum, or by whirling it the way a washing machine whirls wet clothes during the spin cycle.

Next, some plants send the sludge to an enormous sealed tank, called an anaerobic (AN-uh-RO-bik) digester, which heats and mixes the sludge. Anaerobic means "without air." In the digester, bacteria that work best *without* oxygen, **anaerobic bacteria,** eat the organic matter in the sludge. They change it into acids, water, and methane, an odorless gas that can actually be used to heat the treatment plant and the sludge in the digester.

Each household sends about five hundred pounds of sludge to the treatment plant each year. The dried sludge (above) is being composted. At this facility, it heats in special trucks (left) to kill any dangerous bacteria.

After about 25 days, the anaerobic bacteria have eaten all the sludge they can. The still-soggy sludge is squeezed tightly between two large moving belts to remove more water. Now the sludge smells a bit less terrible—like a wet diaper. It looks like black mud that has been rolled under a rolling pin. This dried sludge is called **cake.** Cake ends up dumped in special landfills, piled up in specific areas, or burned.

Some sludge has so few harmful bacteria in it that it is safe enough to be recycled. It can be spread on land ruined by industry or added to fields to help crops grow. It's used on non-food crops like cotton or on food crops that will be processed, like sugar beets. It can also be used on lawns, sports fields, and parks.

Some plants have equipment that will compost the sludge, like when household vegetable peelings and grass clippings are put in a bin and allowed to rot. Composting makes sludge decay further, leaving it drier and more sanitary. Composted sludge is safe enough to mix with soil for *all* growing plants, including vegetable gardens.

Sludge can also be used to produce a building material called biobricks. These bricks look like regular bricks and can be used in small building projects.

To complete the drying process, workers mix and turn long piles of sludge.

Composted sludge provides nutrients that plants need to grow.

Wastewater flowing past ultraviolet light

Zap!: Disinfection

The water that flows from the secondary clarifier to the next tank now looks fish-pond green. In most plants, one more thing happens—**disinfection** (dis-in-FEK-shun). In the disinfection basin, any harmful microorganisms still in the water are destroyed.

There are different ways to destroy the microorganisms. In most wastewater treatment plants, a small amount of a chemical called chlorine is added to the water. Chlorine disinfects the wastewater, just as it disinfects water in swimming pools. Too much chlorine in the water can be dangerous, so researchers are looking for other ways to treat the harmful microorganisms.

One such method uses a special kind of light: ultraviolet light. Sun rays contain ultraviolet light, although we can't see it. A row of lights placed in the water gives off ultraviolet rays and makes the microorganisms harmless.

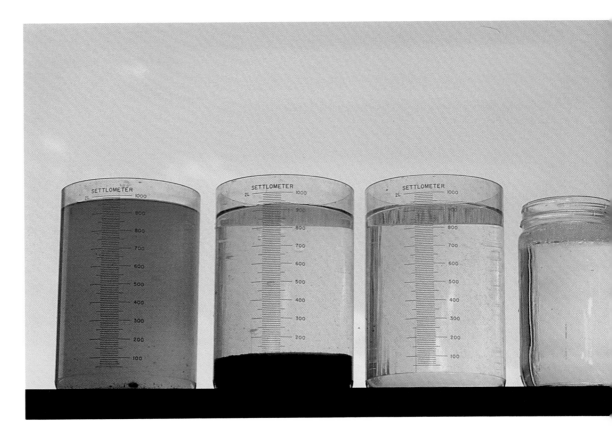

These jars show (from left to right) *water from the aeration basin, water from the secondary clarifier, water after secondary treatment, and tap water.*

Using ultraviolet light to treat bacteria is faster, safer, and works better than using chlorine. It also doesn't add another dangerous chemical that might have to be removed from the water later. The equipment is more expensive to buy, but once installed, it's cheaper to use than chlorine.

After secondary treatment, the wastewater has been in the plant at least eight hours, perhaps as long as sixteen hours. About 85 percent of the solid matter has been removed, but the water often still contains harmful substances.

Since the Clean Water Act requires treatment only to the secondary level, about half of the plants that treat wastewater to this stage now send it to the waterway. In about 40 percent of all plants, however, the water goes through one more stage—**advanced treatment.**

Protecting Nature

Advanced Treatment

Two elements that usually stay in the water after secondary treatment are phosphorus (FAHS-fuhr-uhs) and nitrogen (NY-truh-jun). Phosphorus and nitrogen cause tiny organisms called algae to grow in waterways. Algae grow quickly, then use up oxygen as they die and decay, so little oxygen is left for fish and water plants.

Toxic chemicals and metals from industry and farming that get into the wastewater can also harm fish and water plants. Industries are not usually allowed to send their wastewater into a city's sewer system, so most industries treat the water themselves, then reuse it or send it directly into the waterway.

The algae on this pond are natural and often harmless plants, but when extra nitrogen and phosphorus are added to the water, algae grow faster and use more than their share of oxygen.

These wastewater testers check the wastewater leaving a candy factory before it flows into the sewer system.

A machine takes samples of the candy factory's wastewater every hour.

If an industry is permitted to use the sewer system, it must remove some of the harmful substances from the water before it leaves the factory. But some poisons from industries still end up at the treatment plant along with insect and weed killers from yards and fields. Some plants use advanced treatment to try to take these substances out of the water.

Scrub, Scrub, Scrub

Some advanced treatments are simple. One method sends the water through a filter, often sand or coal. Any bits of matter left in the water are caught in the filter.

Other treatments are more complicated. One method involves adding more chemicals to make the chemicals still in the water clump together and sink. Another uses bacteria to change the chemicals into something harmless. One forces the water through very thin sheets of material that trap the dissolved solids.

These are only a few methods to provide advanced treatment. Different methods are used, depending upon what is still in the water.

Advanced treatment systems, like this sand filter, remove from the water as much of the remaining substances as possible.

A polluted pond

As our water becomes polluted by industry and a rising population, more cities are adding advanced treatment systems to their plants. But advanced treatment has its disadvantages. Because it can remove up to 99 percent of all matter from wastewater, it creates more sludge to dispose of. And, unfortunately, advanced treatment is very expensive. Sometimes it costs as much as all the other treatments combined. Nevertheless, many people who are concerned about the environment believe that all water should get advanced treatment. Someday, it might even be the law.

Clean Enough at Last

Discharge

After its last treatment, the wastewater flows into a pipe that will take it to the outfall. Outfall is the place where the treated water, or **effluent** (EF-loo-ent) goes back into the waterway. This pipe can be as wide as 12 feet across and can reach as far as 10 miles out from shore. The farther out the pipe goes, the safer the beaches and swimming areas are from pollution, especially if the water has had only primary treatment.

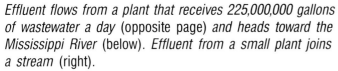

Effluent flows from a plant that receives 225,000,000 gallons of wastewater a day (opposite page) and heads toward the Mississippi River (below). Effluent from a small plant joins a stream (right).

Every day, a technician tests samples of effluent in the plant laboratory. This isn't the first time the water has been tested. Lab workers test the water at each treatment step to make sure it meets the government standards. If the water samples are not clean enough at any stage, the plant manager has to decide how to improve the treatment.

Lab technicians also test the water near the outfall to be sure it's safe for plants and animals living nearby. The tissue of fish and shellfish are also checked for poisons that might kill the fish or hurt people who eat them.

Scuba divers regularly check outfall pipes for leaks or cracks. If the pipes aren't checked carefully, they might break. That happened in San Diego, California, where the waste-water receives only primary treatment. In February 1992, an outfall pipe broke in at least 19 places. The pollution from this one broken outfall pipe closed four miles of beaches and cost the city 16 million dollars.

A plant worker tests effluent before it leaves the plant for the outfall.

Reclaimed water keeps this golf course in California green.

No Drinking!

Not all treatment plants send all their effluent back into the waterways. Plants that use advanced treatment may produce **reclaimed water.** Reclaimed water can be used immediately to water golf courses, parks, yards, and certain crops, to fight fires, and to make artificial snow for ski slopes.

In areas where freshwater is scarce, such as Windhoek, in Namibia, Africa, water regulations allow people to cook with and drink reclaimed water. In the United States,

however, water regulations do not yet permit it to be used for drinking or in household chores, although in some office buildings in California reclaimed water is being used to flush toilets. Someday it might be piped into American homes for similar uses. To make sure reclaimed water would be used correctly, it could be tinted with dye. Blue- or pink-tinted water would tell you that the water from that tap is meant for flushing or washing clothes, but not for drinking.

Natural Methods of Treating Wastewater

Some scientists and engineers think we should use nature's methods for the entire job of cleaning our wastewater. In some places, special wastewater systems are letting nature do just that.

Duckweed and Wastewater

A **marsh system** uses large fields of green, growing water plants such as bulrushes, pennywort, duckweed, and cattails to clean the water. First, solids and grit are removed from the wastewater, and chlorine is usually added to destroy any harmful microorganisms.

This marsh system in south central Poland (above right) uses duckweed (right) *to clean bacteria from the water.*

Because of its rapid growth rate, the water hyacinth plant is sometimes thought of as a pest, but not in San Diego. San Diego has a wastewater treatment plant that uses ponds filled with water hyacinths, fish, and crayfish to clean bacteria from the water.

Then the water is sent through a series of marshes where plant roots absorb metals and chemicals, and bacteria living on the roots eat the minerals and organic matter in the water. While they eat, the bacteria make food for the plants they grow on. Together, the plants and the bacteria provide advanced treatment for the water. When the effluent leaves the bird- and fish-filled marshes to return to the waterways, it is sometimes cleaner than the water it is joining.

This rock marsh system for a single home treats wastewater using plants called elephant ears.

Elephant Ears and Canna Lilies

In a **rock marsh system,** the wastewater isn't visible, because layers of small rocks cover the water fields. Water plants grow through the rocks with their roots in the water below. Since sewage-hungry bacteria live on both the rocks and on the plant roots, this system works very well.

In some rock marshes, pretty plants like water irises, elephant ears, and canna lilies act as filters. The plant roots remove toxic chemicals and nitrogen from the water, and except for some chlorine for disinfection, no chemicals are added. The ponds, often filled with blooming flowers, can be beautiful to look at and can become home to fish, birds, and animals.

Compared to standard treatment plants, marsh systems are inexpensive to build and cheaper to maintain. They also smell better—like a natural marsh. Unfortunately, marsh systems don't work in areas where cold weather would kill the plants. But there is another wastewater system being developed that will work in any area, regardless of the temperature outside.

A rock marsh system using canna lilies cleans the wastewater for this mobile home park.

Solar aquatics systems can look like gardens.

Let the Sun Shine In

Solar aquatics is a treatment system in which sunshine (solar) and water (aquatics) come together. A solar aquatics system uses water plants to clean wastewater, just like a marsh system, but here the plants grow in clear, plastic tanks of water inside a glass building called a greenhouse. Solar aquatics needs no more land than a standard treatment plant and costs less to operate, and since it's indoors, it can be used in cold climates.

Rock marshes and solar aquatics have not been tested as thoroughly as standard treatment plant methods. But since these natural systems give wastewater an effective advanced treatment, they are important to the future of wastewater management. Advanced treatment is becoming essential to keeping our waterways clean.

Too Precious to Waste

Nowadays people are boating and fishing again on the Cuyahoga River. Thanks to better pollution control and wastewater treatment, it should never again catch fire. But the earth's water still isn't as clean as it should be. It needs protecting if we are to have enough safe water for everyone.

Wastewater treatment systems are a necessary and intelligent way to protect our water. Another way is for everyone to treat water wisely from the moment it pours out of the faucet—by using only what is needed and by keeping it free of pollution.

There is only a small amount of usable water on the earth. The water we wash in today must be used over and over by others in the future. We must do what we can to protect it.

The Cuyahoga River in Cleveland, Ohio, is once again a place for recreation.

Caution! What's Going down the Drain?

You can help your wastewater treatment plant.

• Be careful what you put down the drain. Bug killer, paint thinner, and other dangerous fluids are difficult for treatment plants to remove from wastewater.

• Dumping harmful chemicals on the ground isn't safe either. Fertilizer and weed killer used on lawns and gardens may be washed into the sewer and sent to the treatment plant. These chemicals are difficult to clean from the water, too.

• Most communities have special places to dispose of harmful chemicals. Find out where your family can take empty containers of toxic liquids or used car oil.

• Treatment plants spend a lot of time cleaning water that hasn't even been used. You can help by sending less water down the drain.

• Take short showers or shallow baths.

• Make sure you turn the tap off all the way. One tap dripping twice a second will send over 50 gallons of *clean* water to the treatment plant each week. If you see a leaky tap, tell someone who can fix it.

• Turn off the water while you're brushing your teeth, washing your hands, or washing the car.

• Keep drinking water in the refrigerator so you don't have to run the tap to get cold water.

• Don't use the toilet as a garbage can. It takes five to eight gallons of water to flush a nose-blowing tissue down the toilet.

• Use a broom, not a hose, to clean the sidewalk or driveway.

• Encourage your family to start a backyard compost pile, instead of putting kitchen wastes down a garbage disposal that needs running water to work. This saves water *and* sends less organic matter to the treatment plant.

Fun Flushing Facts

Where a family's wastewater comes from:
Toilet: 33%
Clothes washing: 26%
Bathing: 19.6%
Bathroom sink: 11.3%
Kitchen sink: 5.8%
Dishwashing (automatic): 2.5%
Garbage disposal (grinding): 1.8%

Gallons of water flushed in the United States daily: 4,800,000,000 (That's right, 4.8 billion!)
Gallons that would be flushed if all toilets were replaced with low-flush toilets: 1,536,000,000
Amount of water that would be saved: 3,264,000,000 gallons, or 68%

Chemicals that help lawns grow are difficult for treatment plants to remove from wastewater.

Amount of toilet paper used in the United States every year: 22,627 square miles (That would cover nearly all of West Virginia!)

Amount of toothpaste used in the United States in one day: 550,000 pounds, the weight of about 275 elephants

Amount of money spent every year on chemicals to make American toilets smell better: $9,800,000

Amount of urine Americans pass daily: 88,000,000 gallons

Amount of mouthwash gargled every day in the United States and then washed down the drain: 69,000 gallons

Amount of water used in one day in the United States: 450,000,000,000 gallons (That's enough to fill a swimming pool nine stories deep and the size of Manhattan, New York. It's also 3 times as much as is used in Japan, 70 times as much as used in Ghana, West Africa, and 2 to 4 times as much as is used in all of Europe each day.)

Amount of fresh drinking water Americans need every day: 115,000,000 gallons (That's equal to about 1.84 billion glasses of milk.)

Glossary

advanced treatment: a wastewater treatment that goes a step beyond secondary treatment in order to remove such things as phosphorus, nitrogen, and any remaining solids

aerobic bacteria: microorganisms that live naturally in all water. They need oxygen to live and work.

anaerobic bacteria: microorganisms that do not need oxygen to live and work.

bacteria: microscopic-sized one-celled organisms. There are helpful and harmful bacteria.

cake: sludge with some water removed. Cake that meets government rules can be recycled.

disinfection: the adding of chlorine or ultraviolet light to treated water to make any microorganisms still in the water harmless

effluent: the treated wastewater that comes out of a treatment plant

influent: the untreated wastewater coming into a treatment plant

inorganic matter: matter that does not come from plants or animals. Sand, gravel, and iron are inorganic.

marsh system: a natural water treatment system that uses growing plants and bacteria in the water to remove wastes

microorganism: a living being too tiny to be seen except under a microscope. There are helpful and harmful microorganisms. Harmful microorganisms can make people sick. Some helpful microorganisms clean wastewater. (See also aerobic and anaerobic bacteria.)

organic matter: matter that comes from plants or animals. Leaves, roots, and hair are organic.

primary treatment: wastewater treatment during which 40 to 50 percent of the solids are removed from the water by allowing them to settle out

reclaimed water: treated water that is safe enough to swim in and not make you sick if you accidentally swallow some. In the United States, it is not used for drinking or household chores.

rock marsh system: a natural water treatment system in which rocks cover fields of wastewater. Plants living in the water and bacteria living on the plant roots and on the rocks clean the wastewater.

secondary treatment: the stage of wastewater treatment in which bacteria remove about 85 percent of the solids from the water

septic system: a small system used to treat the wastewater from one building. The wastewater flows into an underground tank and then into pipes that are full of holes. The water is filtered as it dribbles through crushed rock and into the ground. Every few years, the sludge and scum left in the tank are pumped out.

sludge: the thick, watery "solids" removed from wastewater during treatment

solar aquatics: a natural way to treat wastewater using sunshine, plants, and water creatures. Although nature has always used this method to clean water, humans have only recently started building treatment plants that take full advantage of these natural processes.

wastewater: the used water that goes down drains and into the sewer system. It contains human waste as well as detergents, cleaners, pesticides, plastics, paper, and sometimes chemicals from businesses.

waterway: a stream, river, lake, or ocean into which a nearby wastewater treatment plant sends its effluent

Index

Credits

Additional photographs and illustrations courtesy of: The Mansell Collection, p. 10; The Bettman Archive, p. 12 (right), p. 14 (both); Library of Congress, p. 13; Ohio EPA, p. 15 (top), p. 50–51; Kevin A. Kerwin/Regina Villa Associates, p. 15 (bottom); Bryan Liedahl, p. 17 (left); Metropolitan Council Wastewater Services, p. 30 (inset); Jeff Greenberg, p. 38; The F. B. Leopold Company, Inc., p. 40; Minnesota Water and Pollution Control Agency, p. 41, p. 52; Karen Mueller Coombs, p. 45; Lemna Corporation, p. 46 (both), back cover; © Andrew W. Shaw, Jr., p. 47; Wolverton Environmental Services, Inc., Picayune, Mississippi, p. 48, 49 (top); Ocean Arcs International, p. 49 (bottom); additional illustrations by Bryan Liedahl.